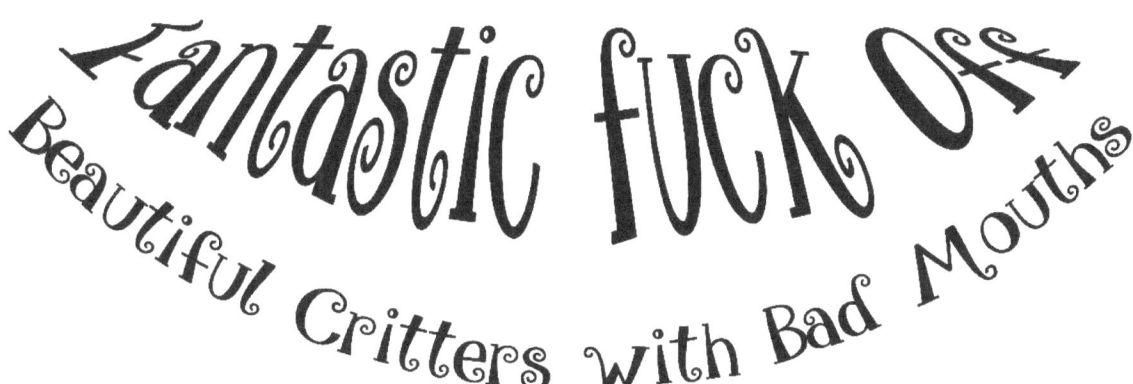

Adult Swear Word Coloring Book

By

S.B. Nozar

Copyright © 2016 by S.B. Nozaz

All rights reserved worldwide. No part of this publication may be reproduced or distributed in any form or by any means, mechanical, electronic or stored in a retrieval or database system, without written permission from the copyright holder.

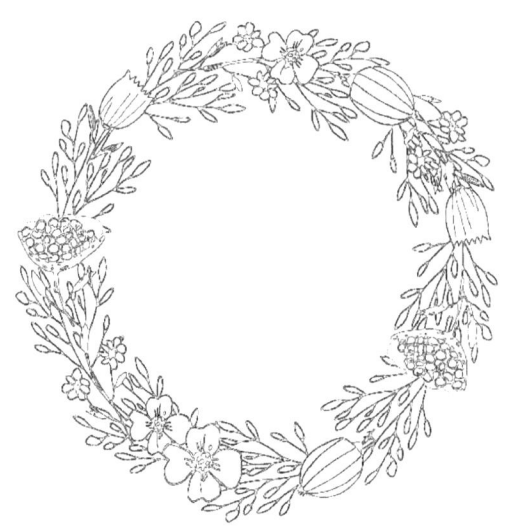

Happy Coloring!

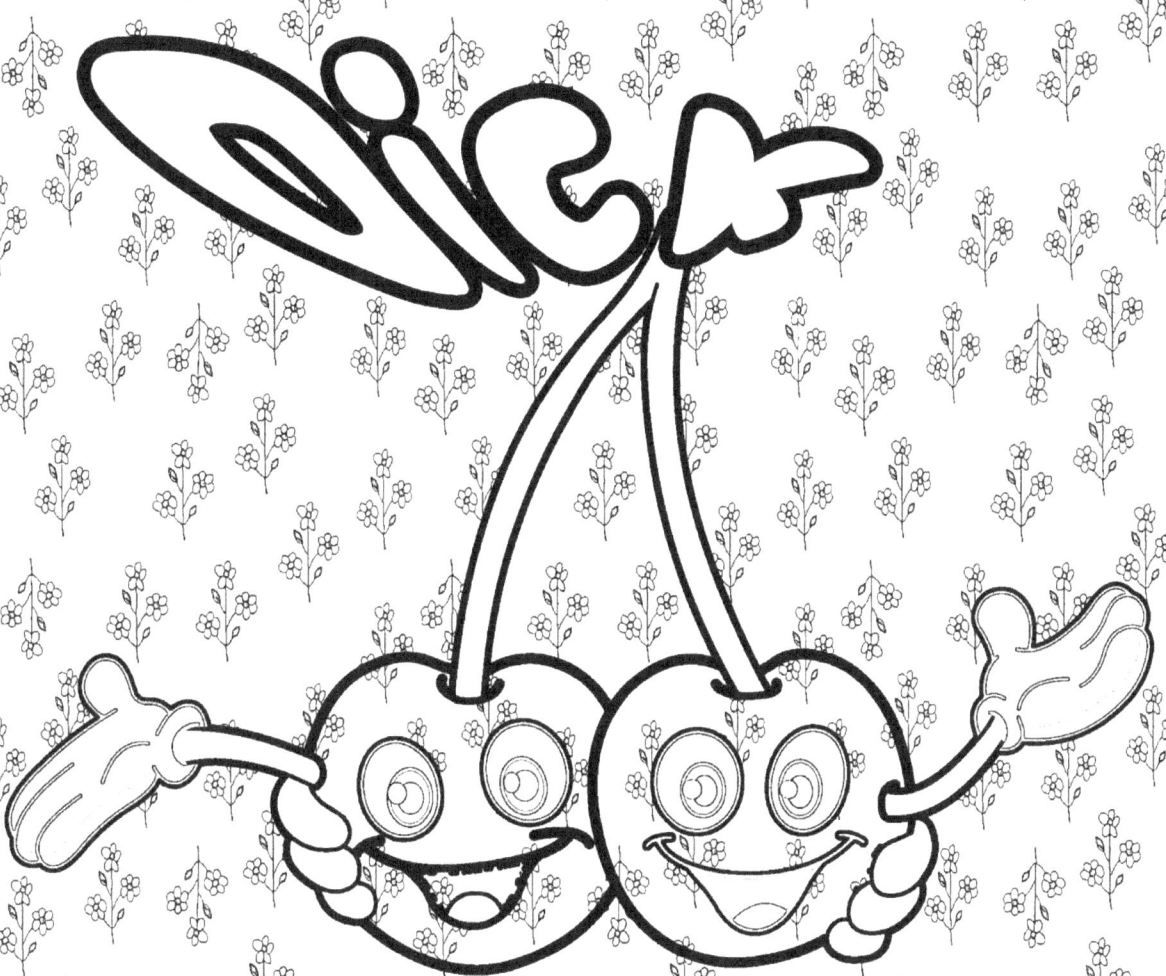

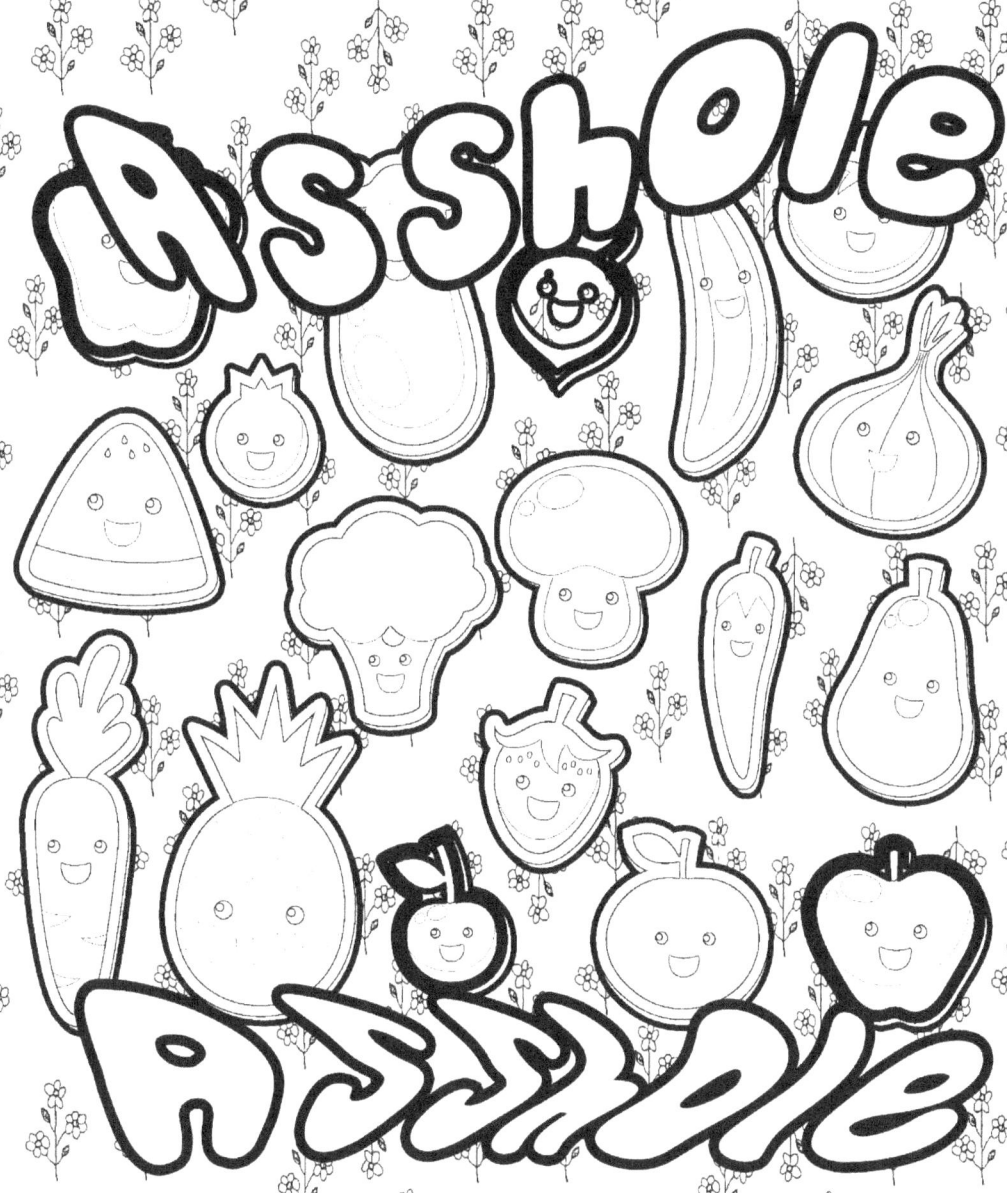

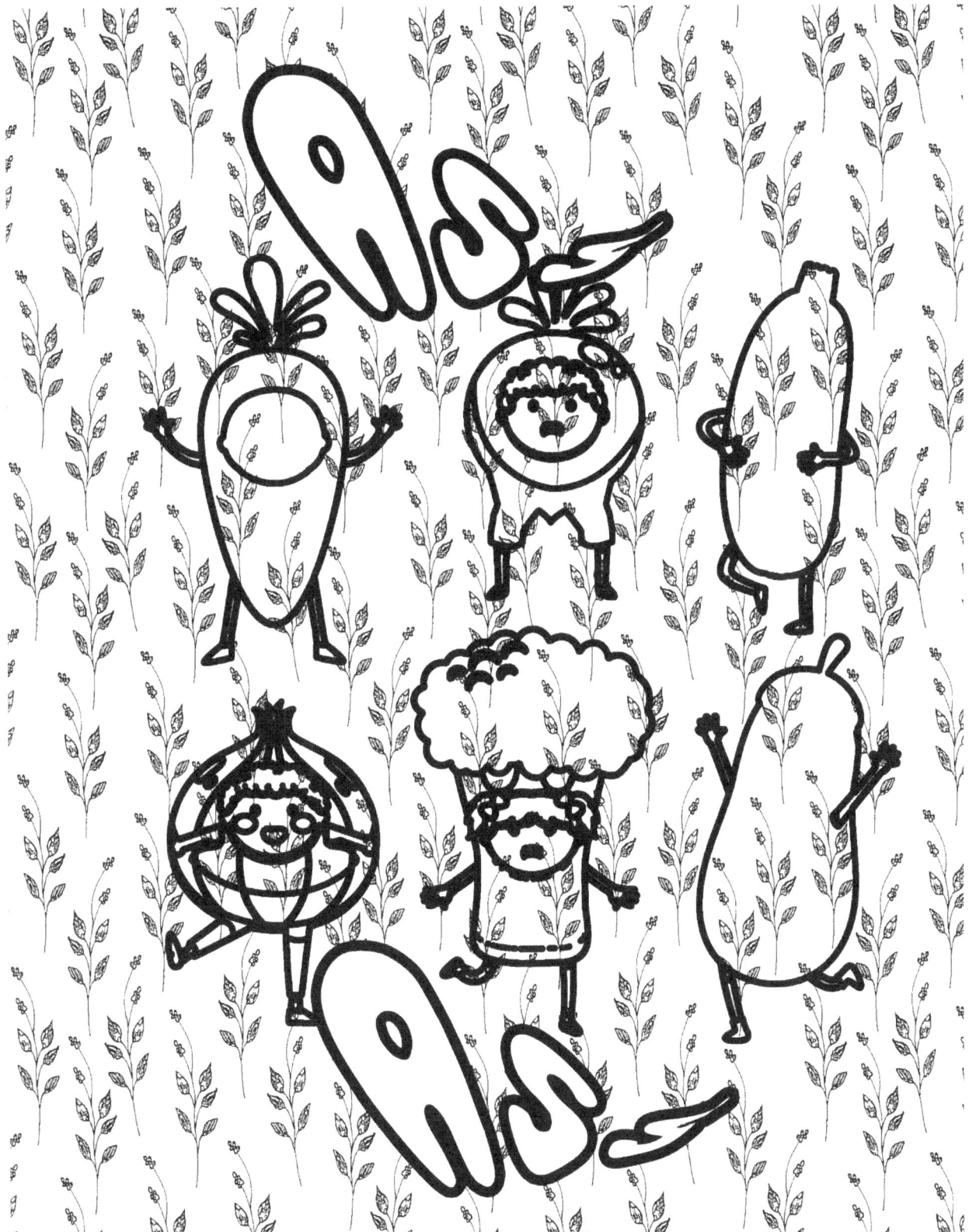

Doucheb@9

Doucheb@9

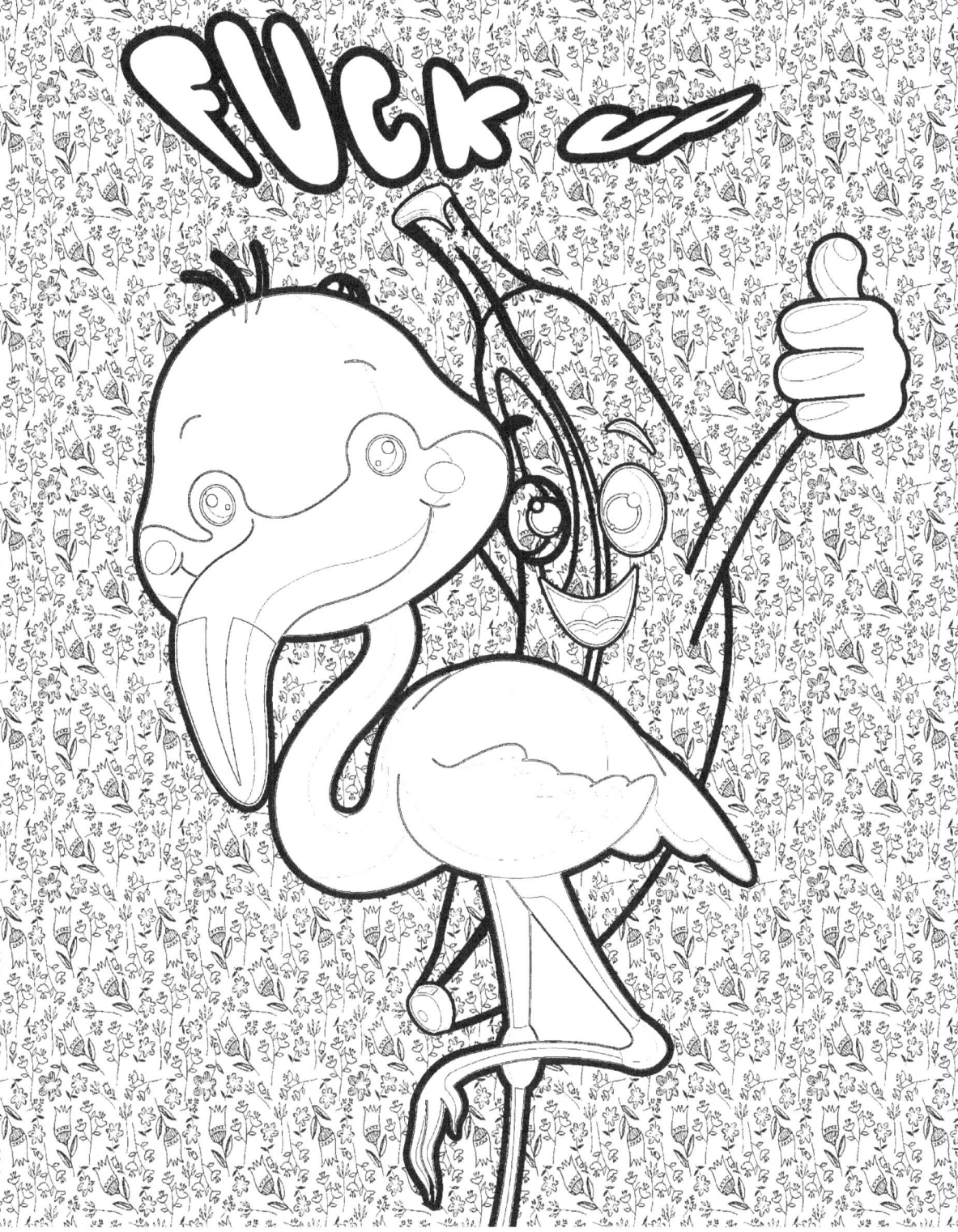

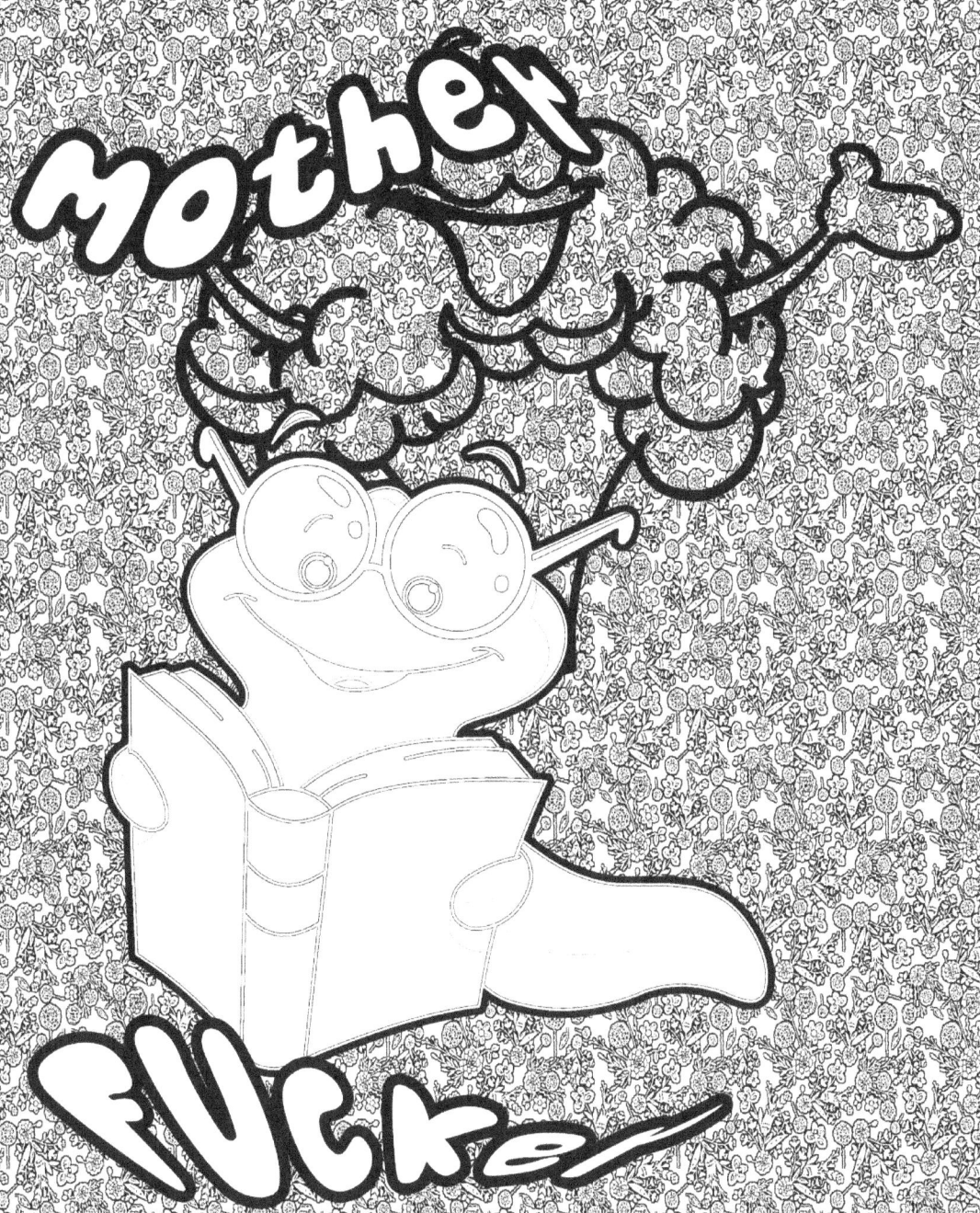

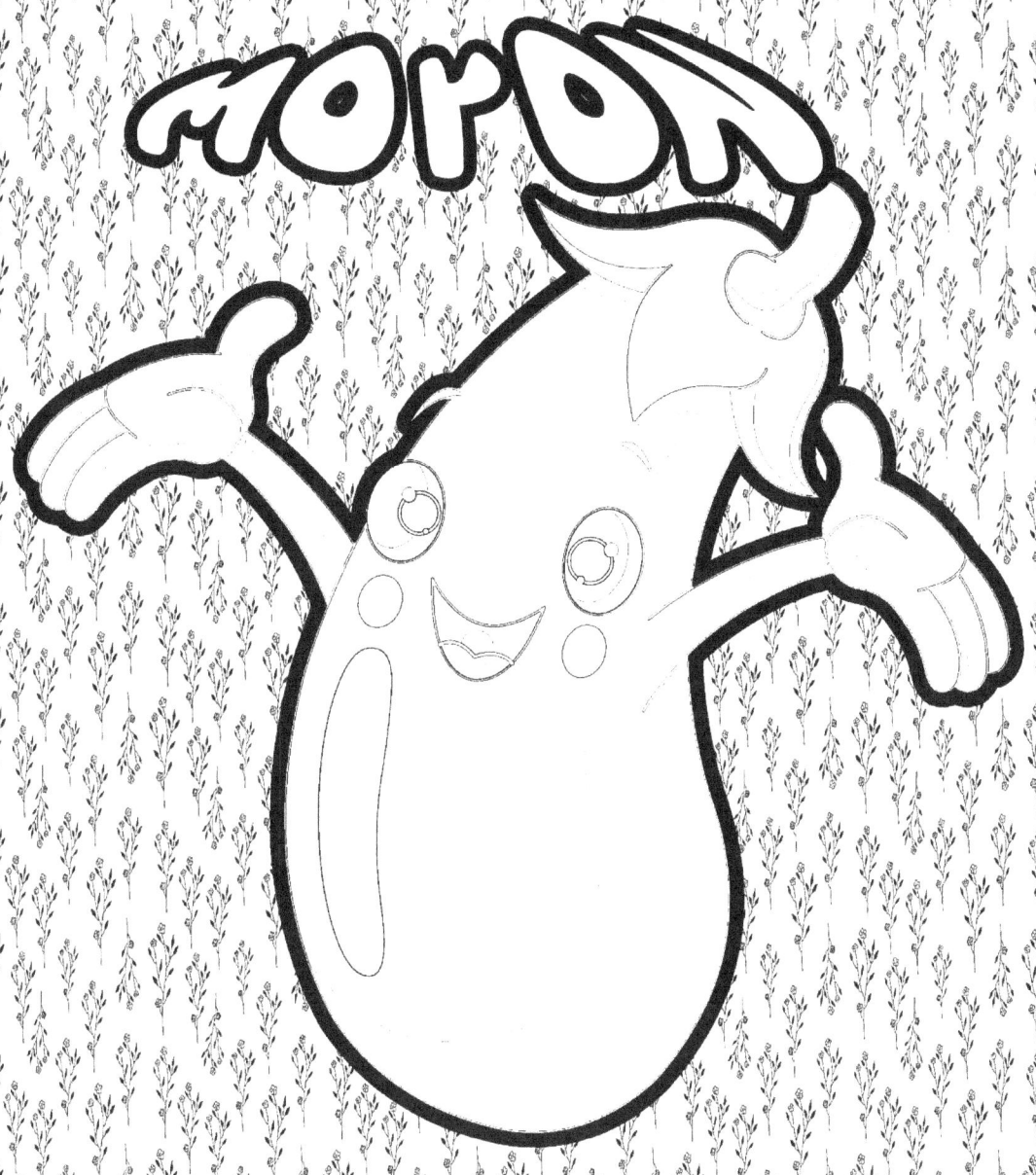

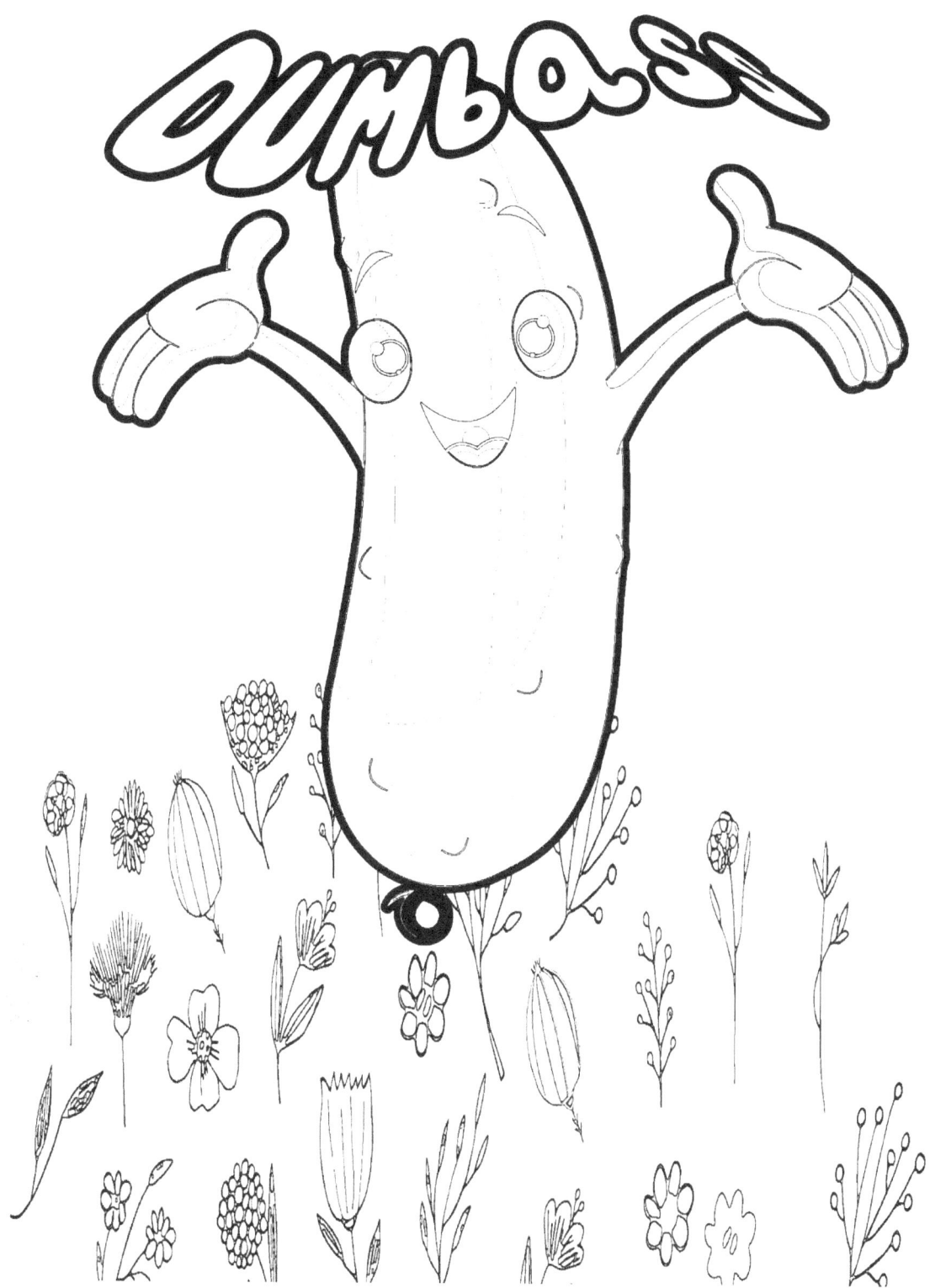

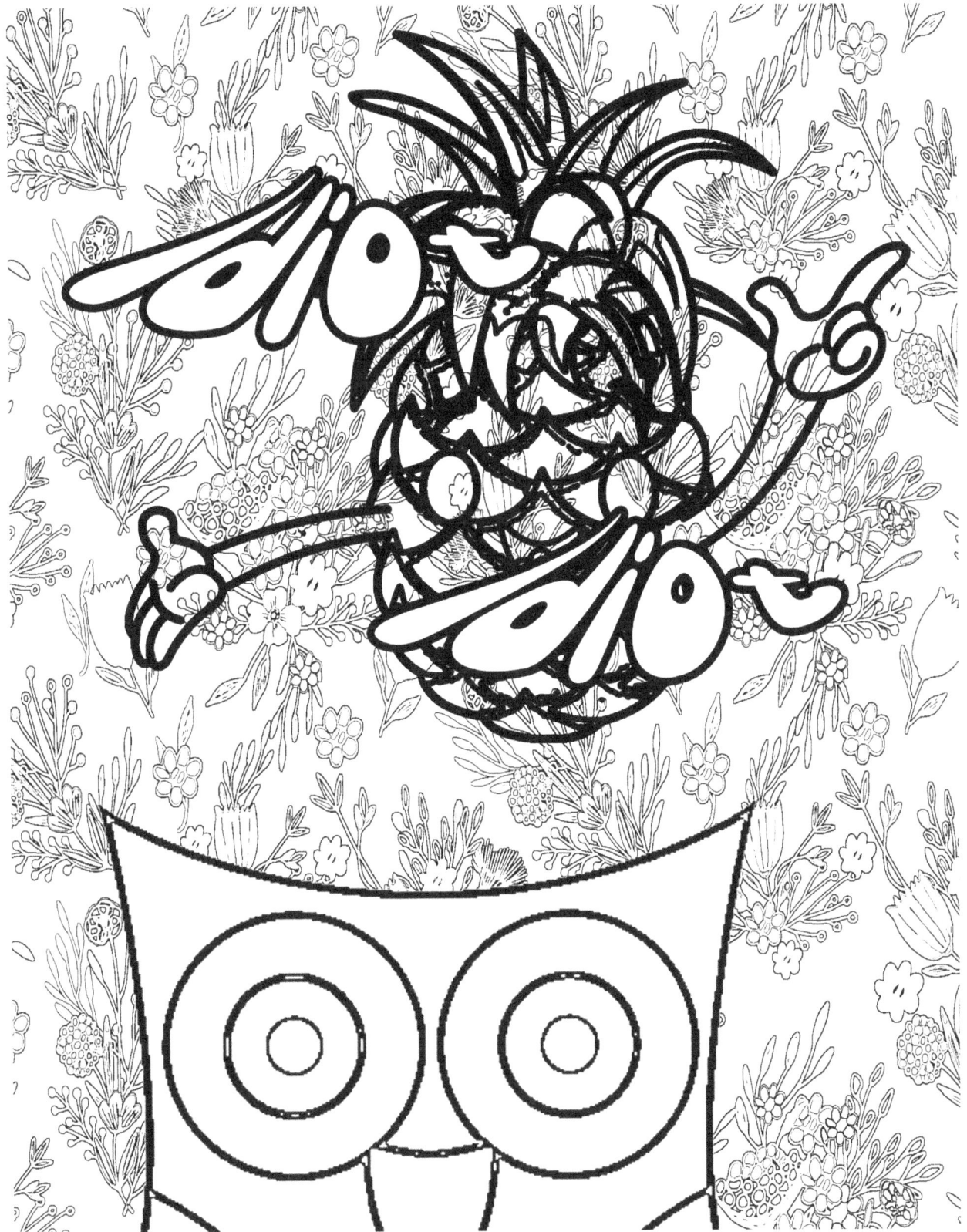

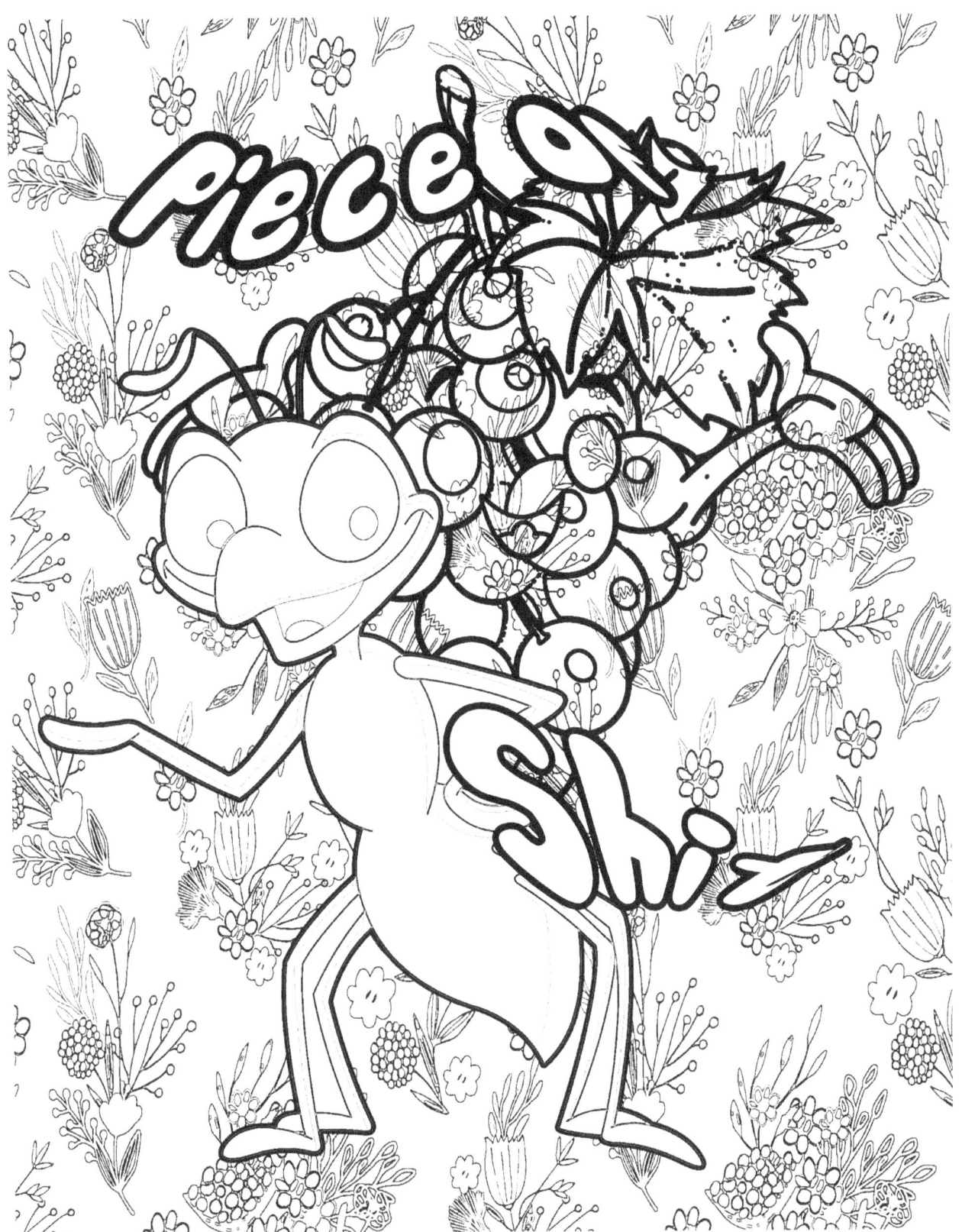

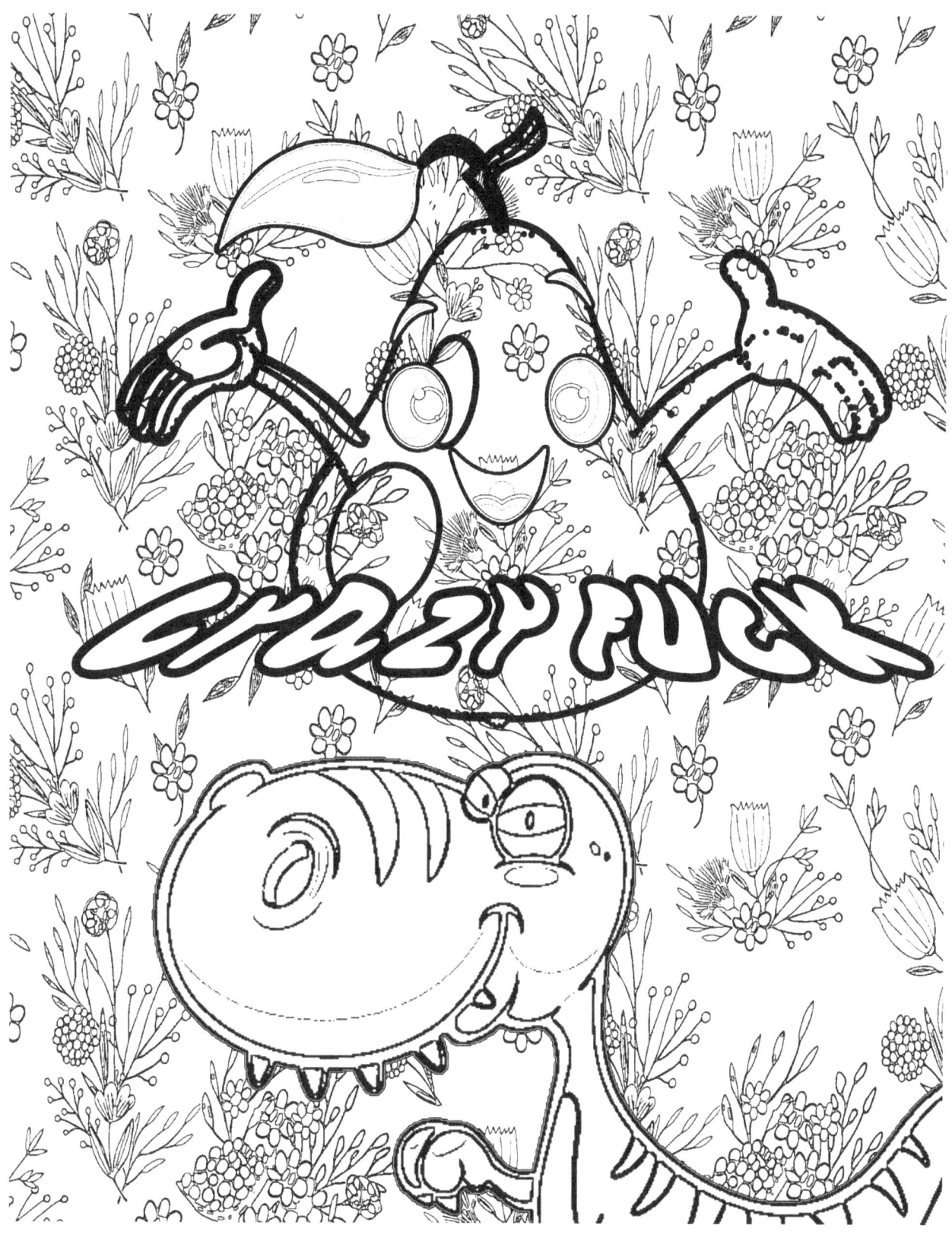

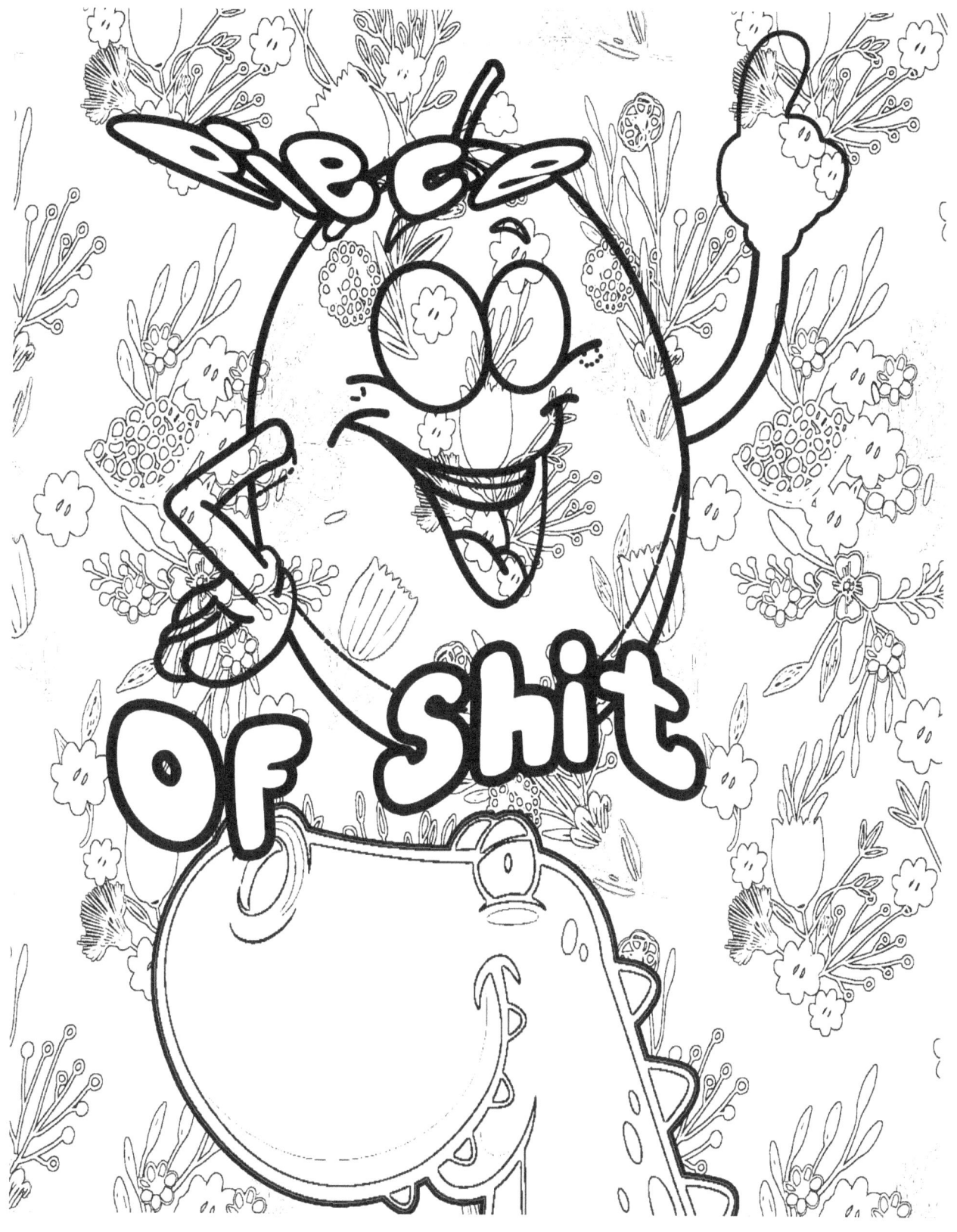

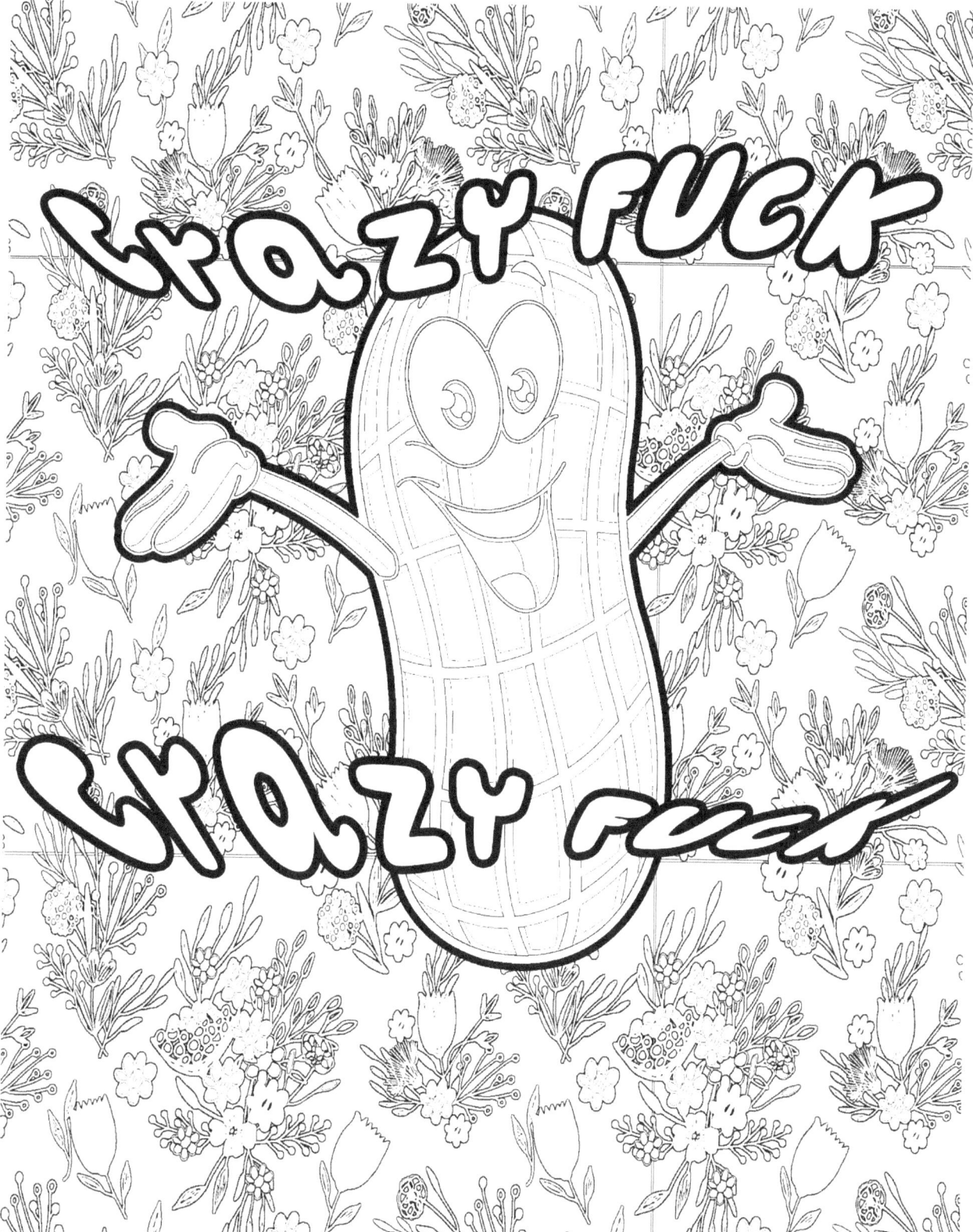

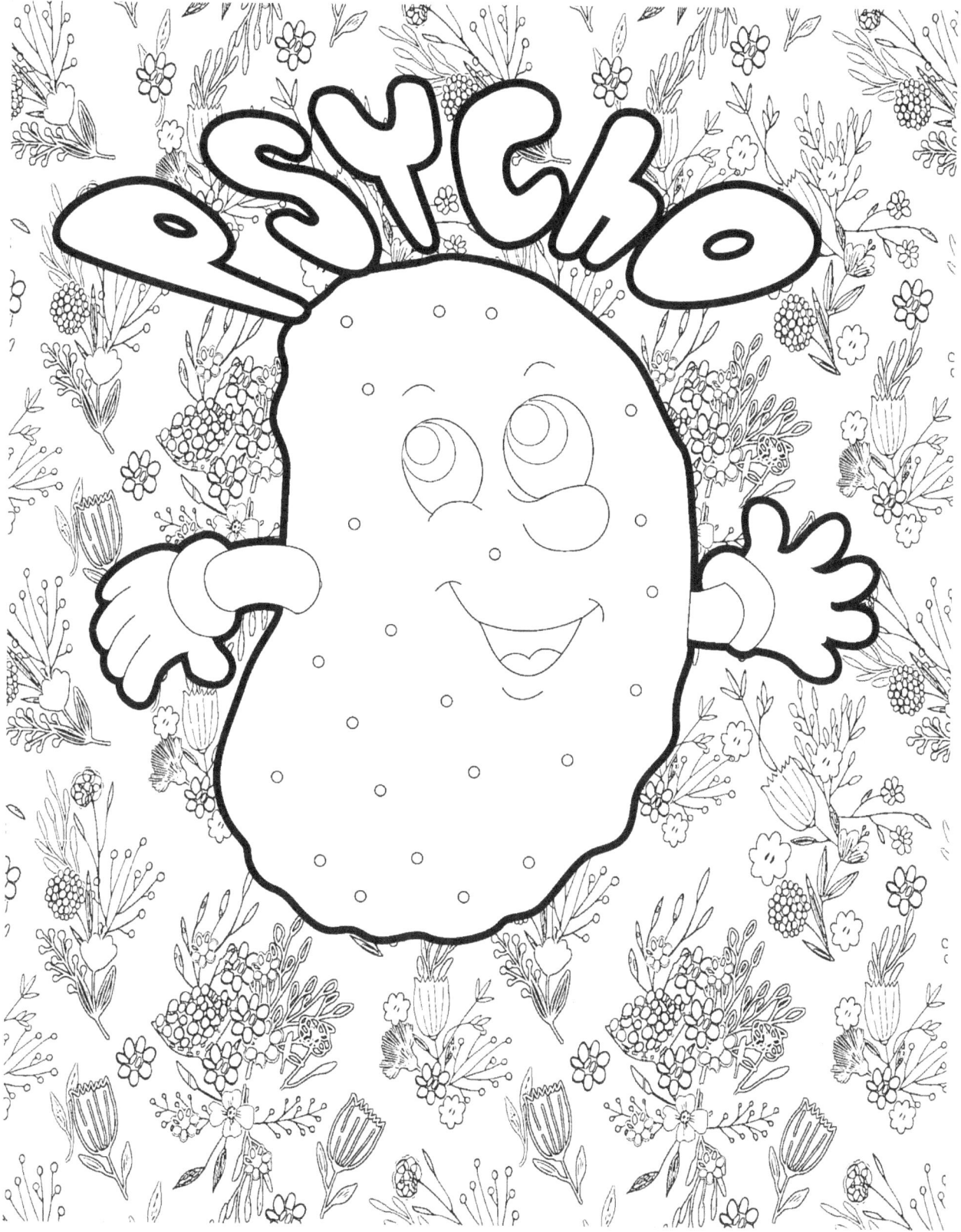

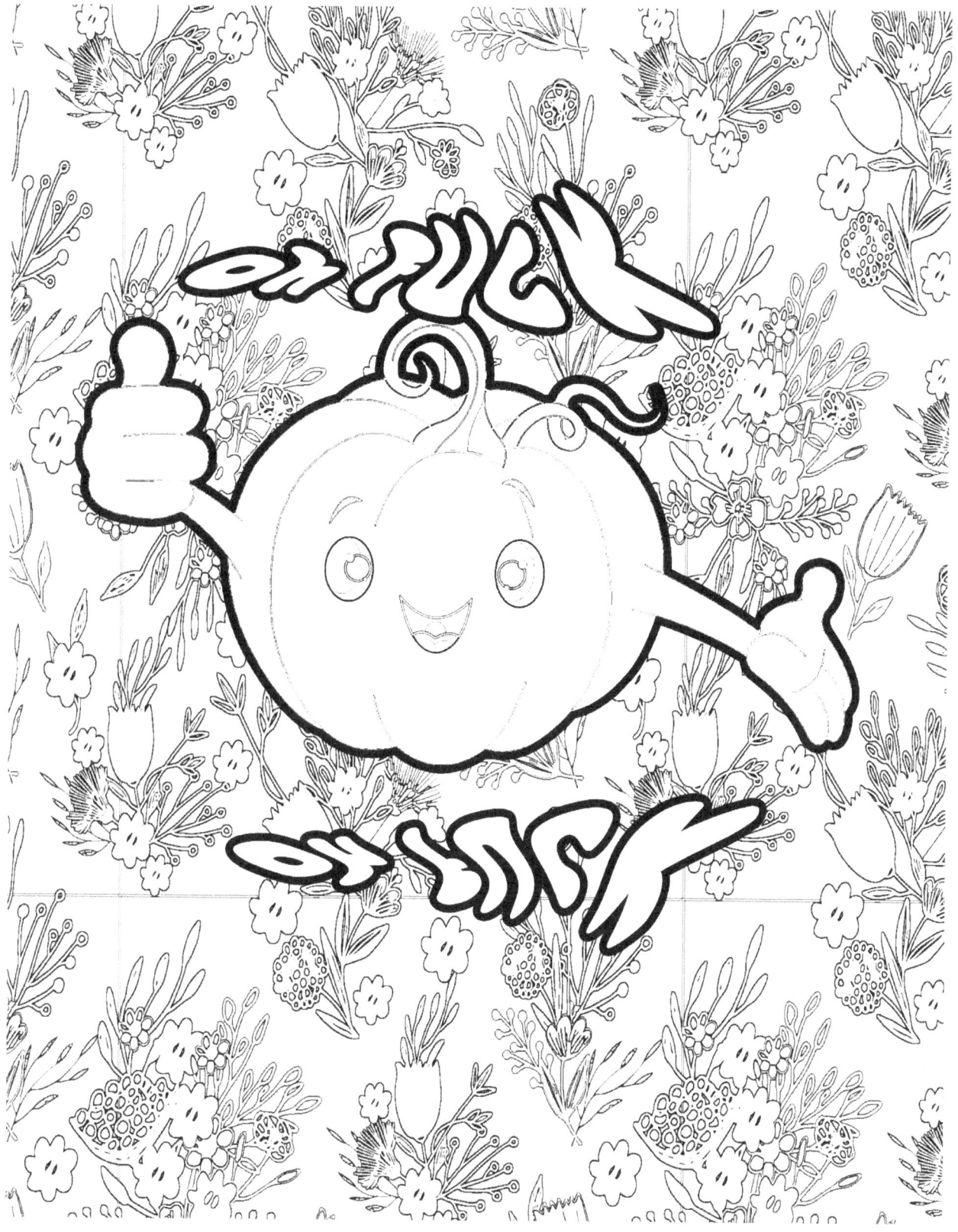

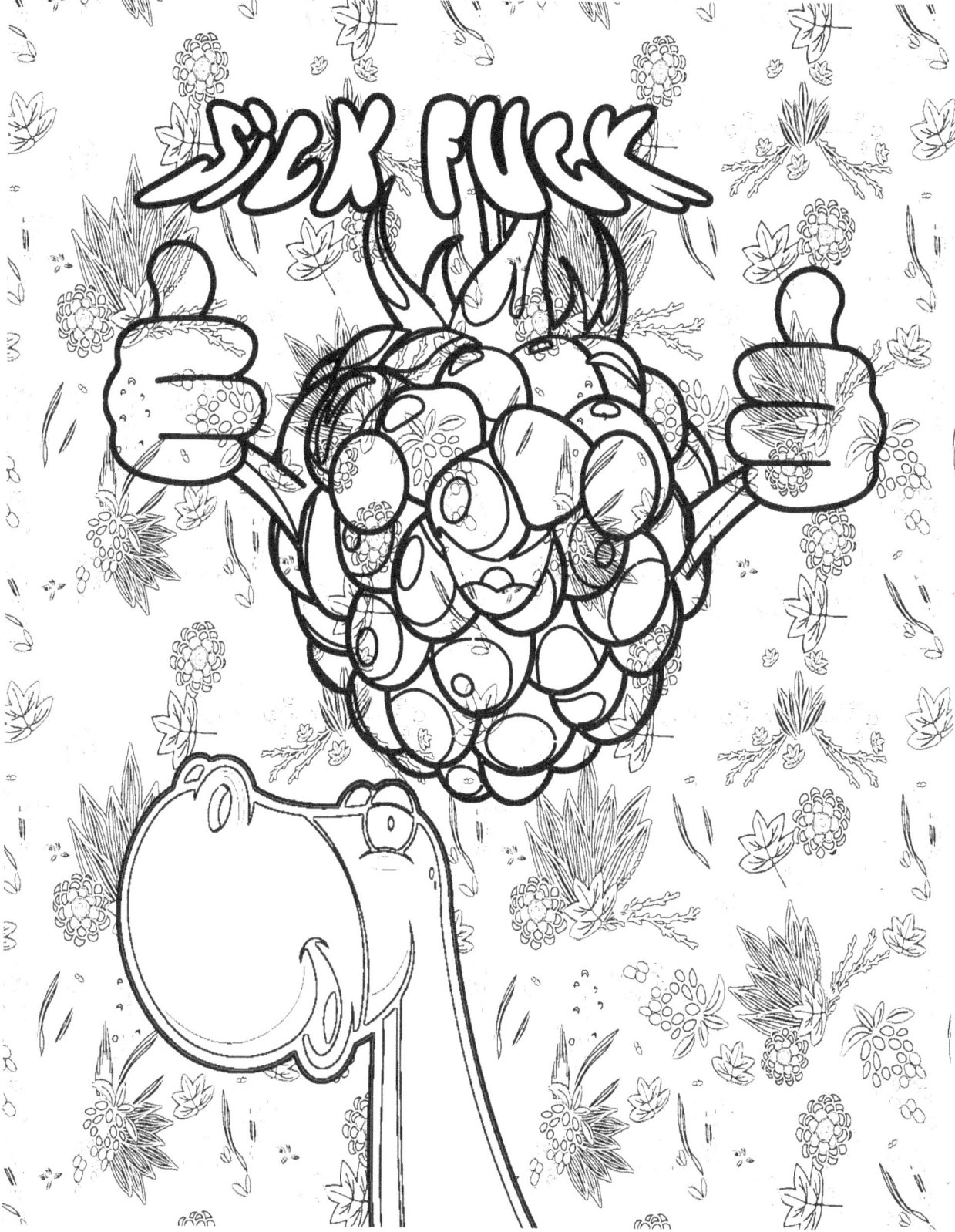

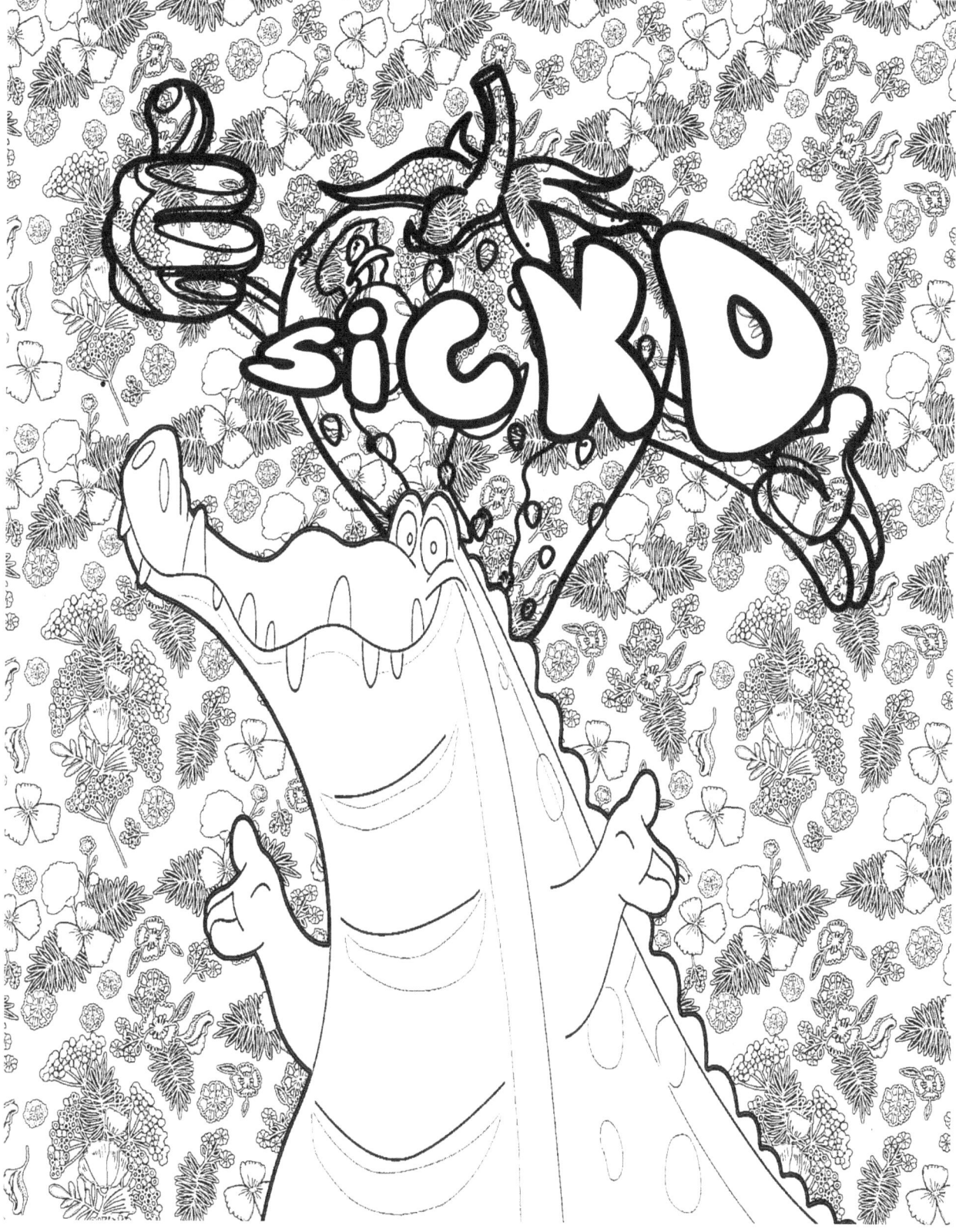

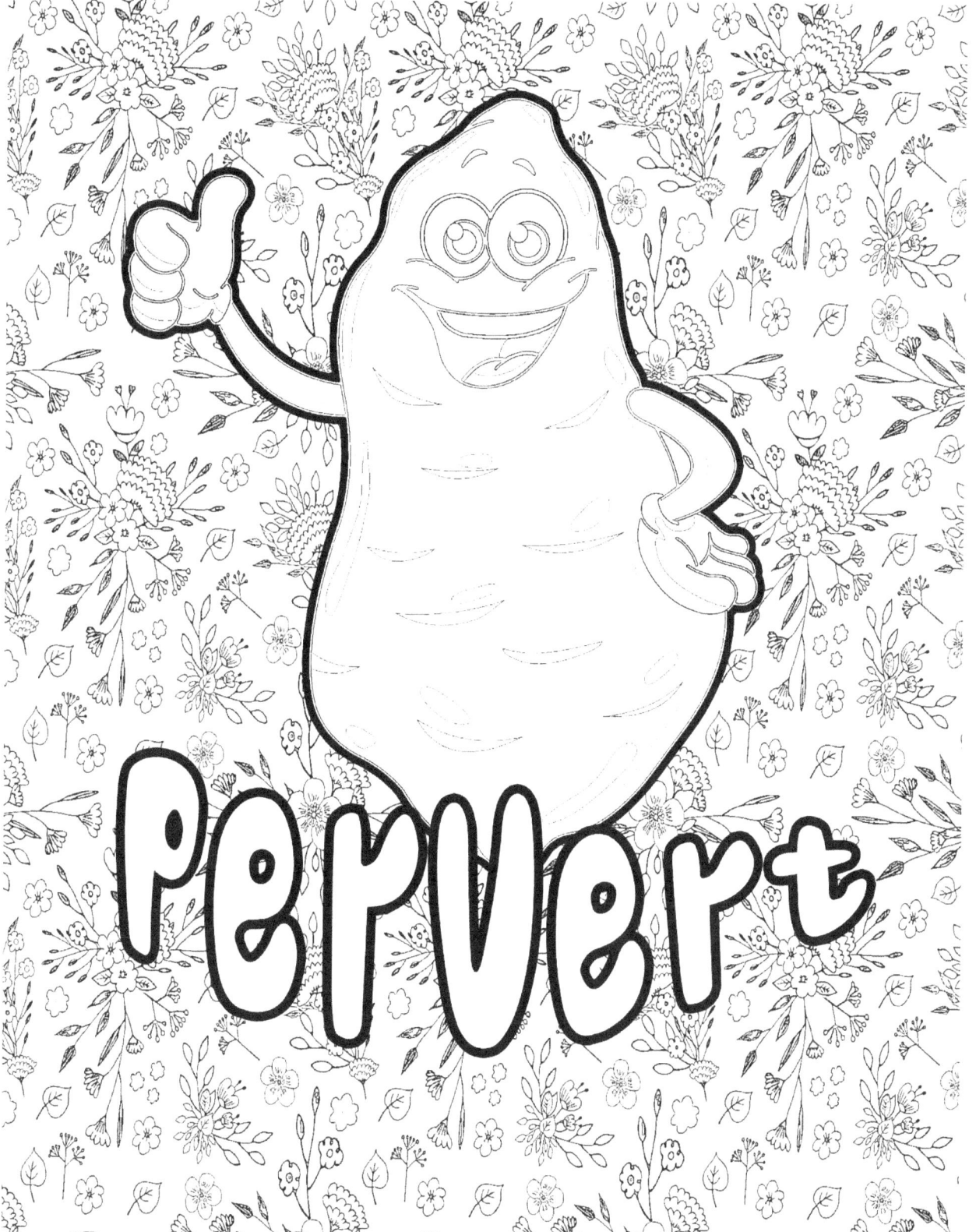

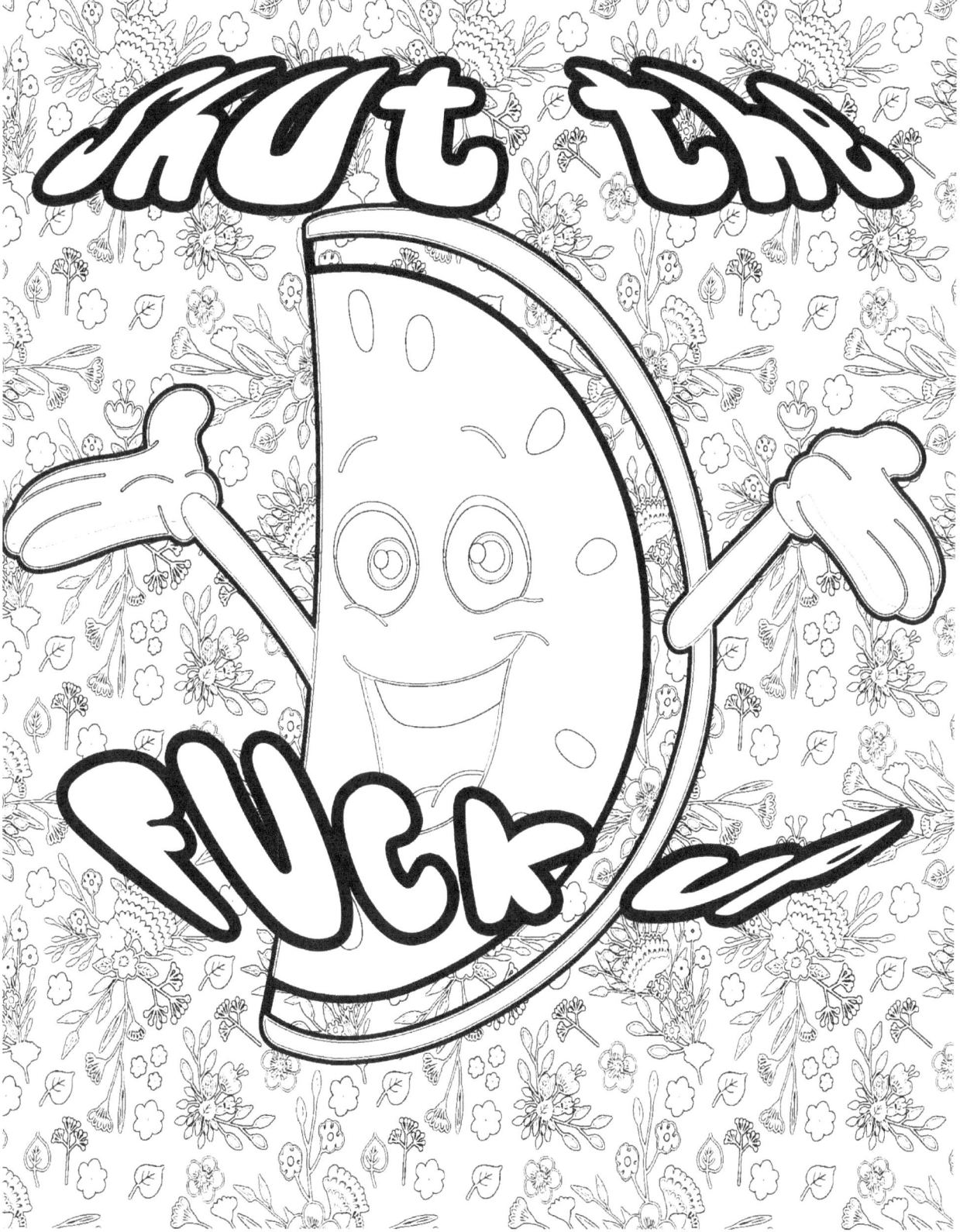

stUpid

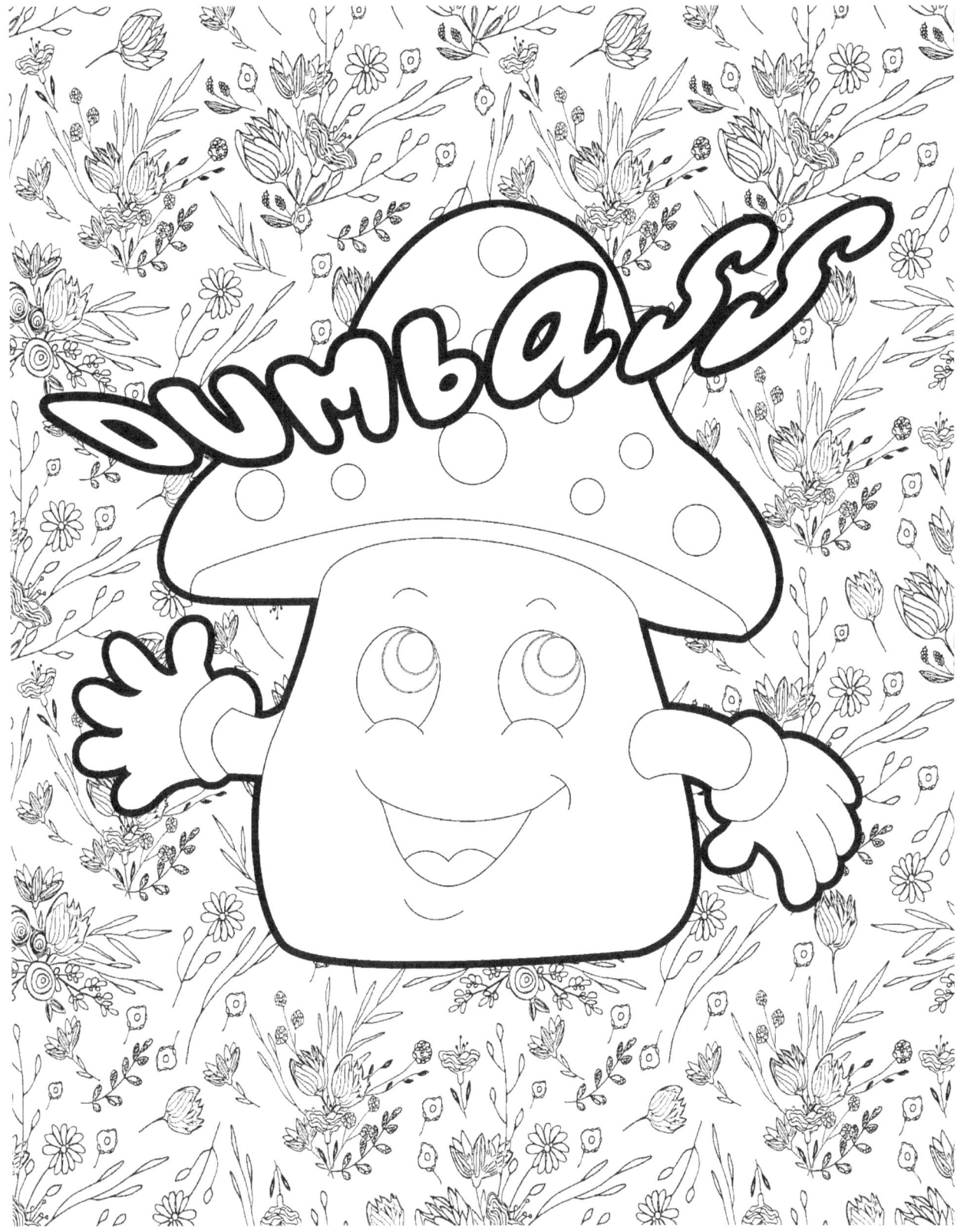

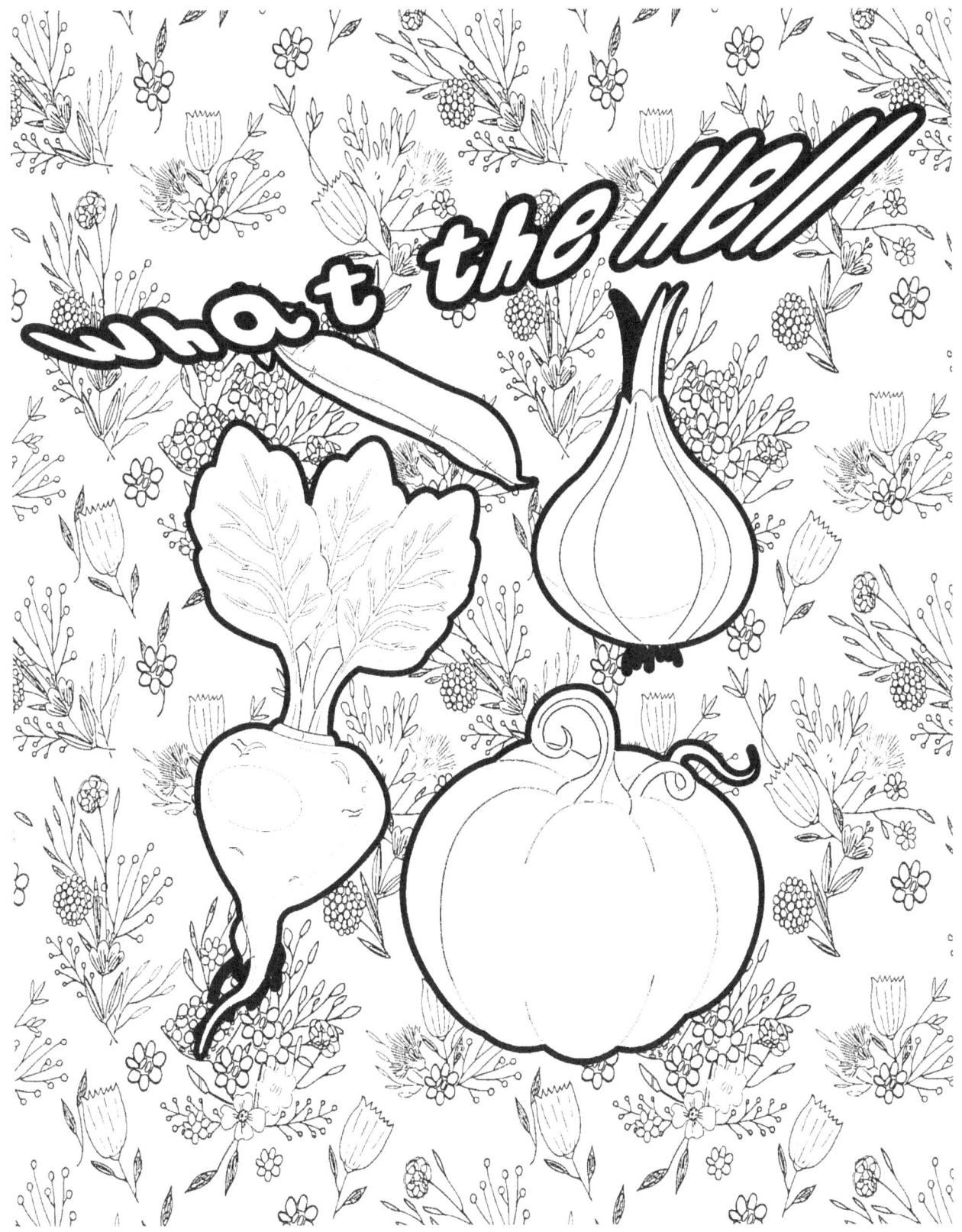

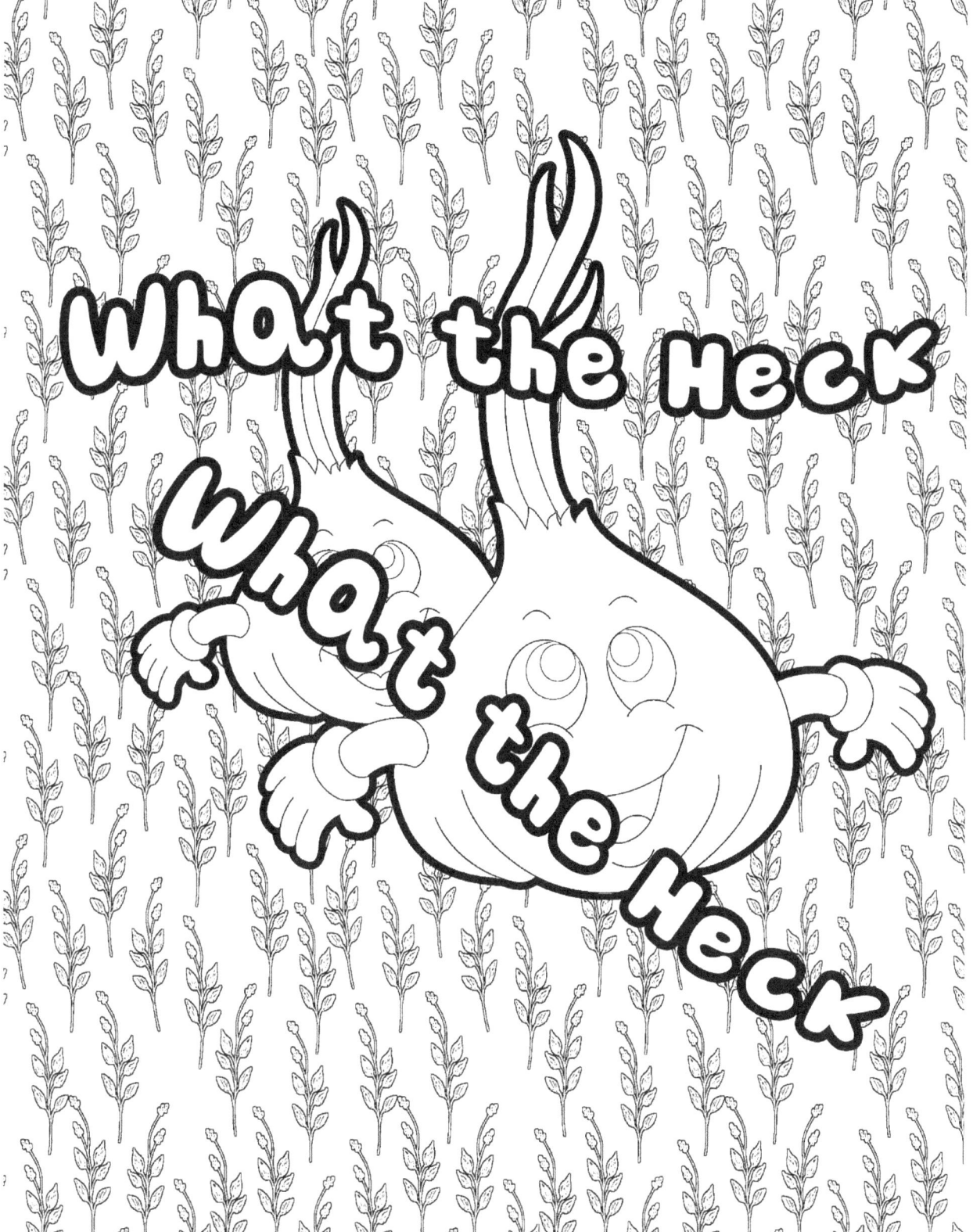

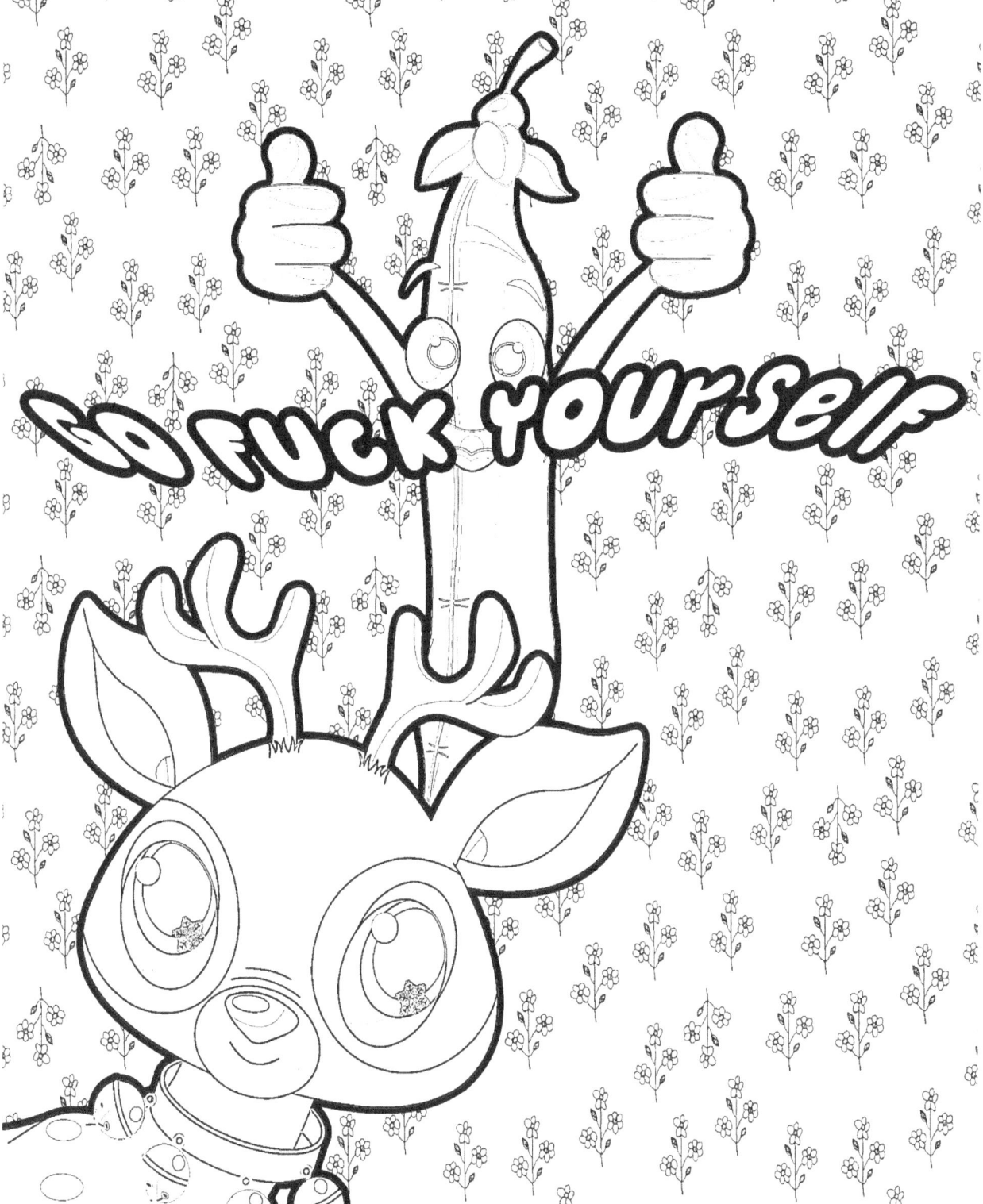

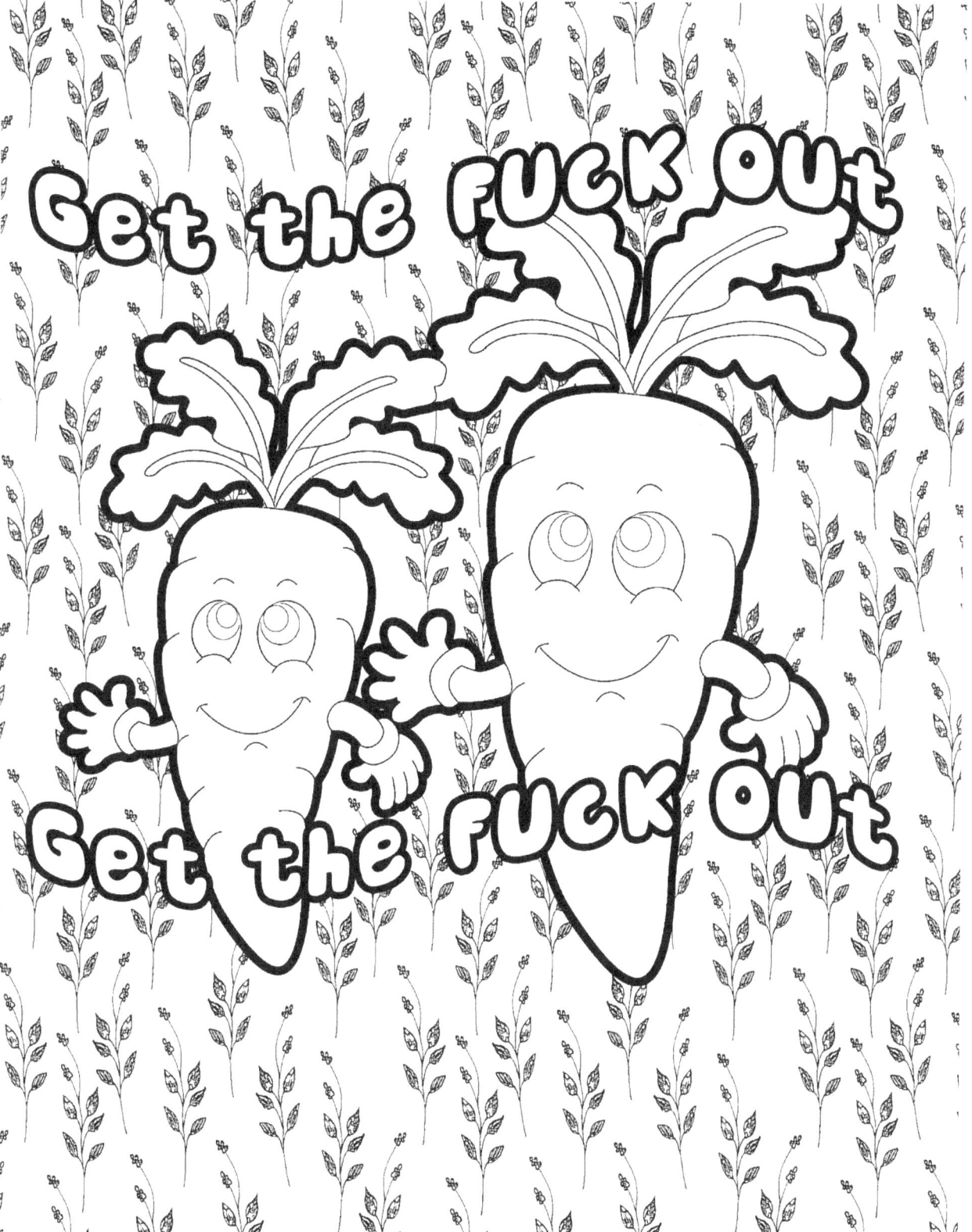

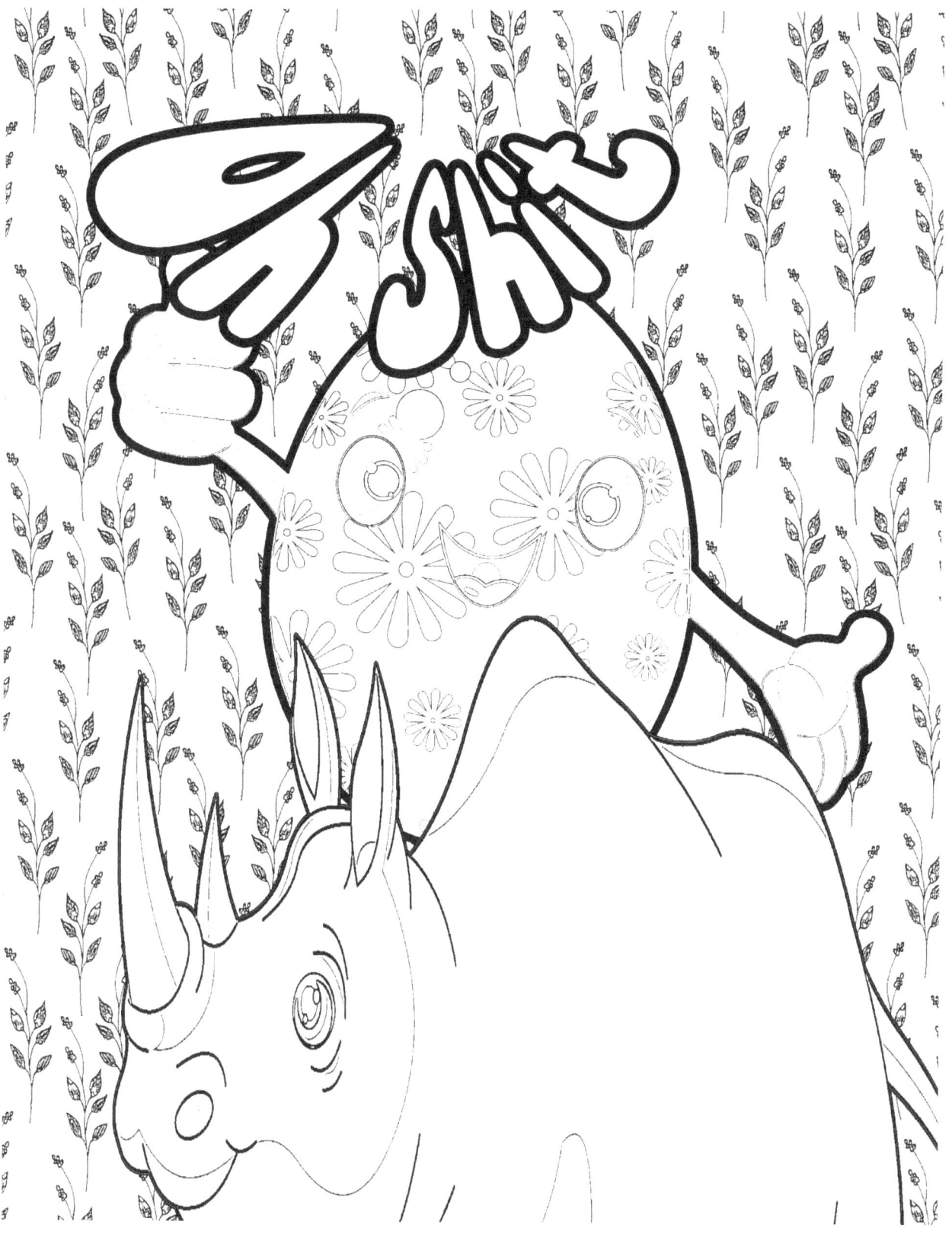

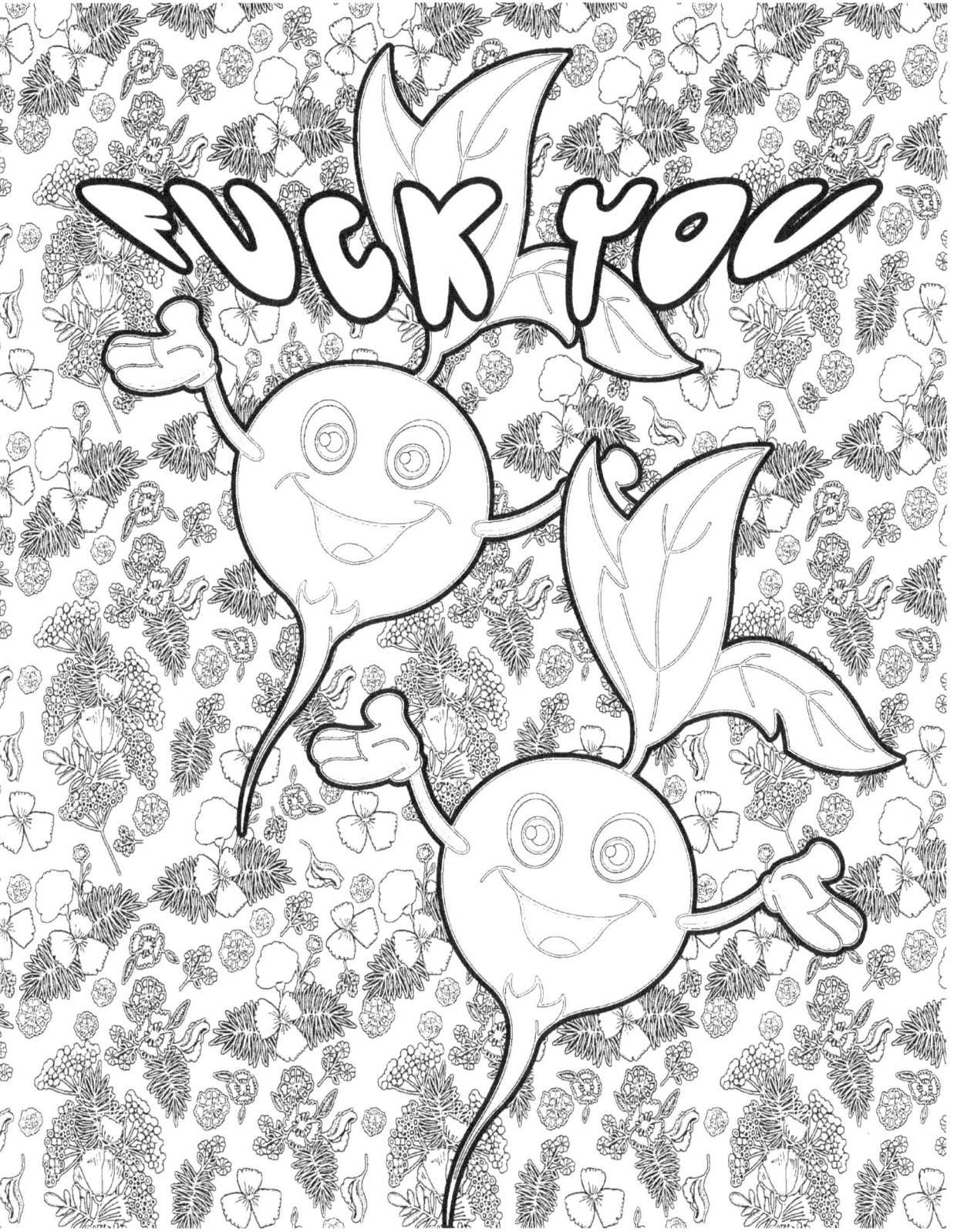

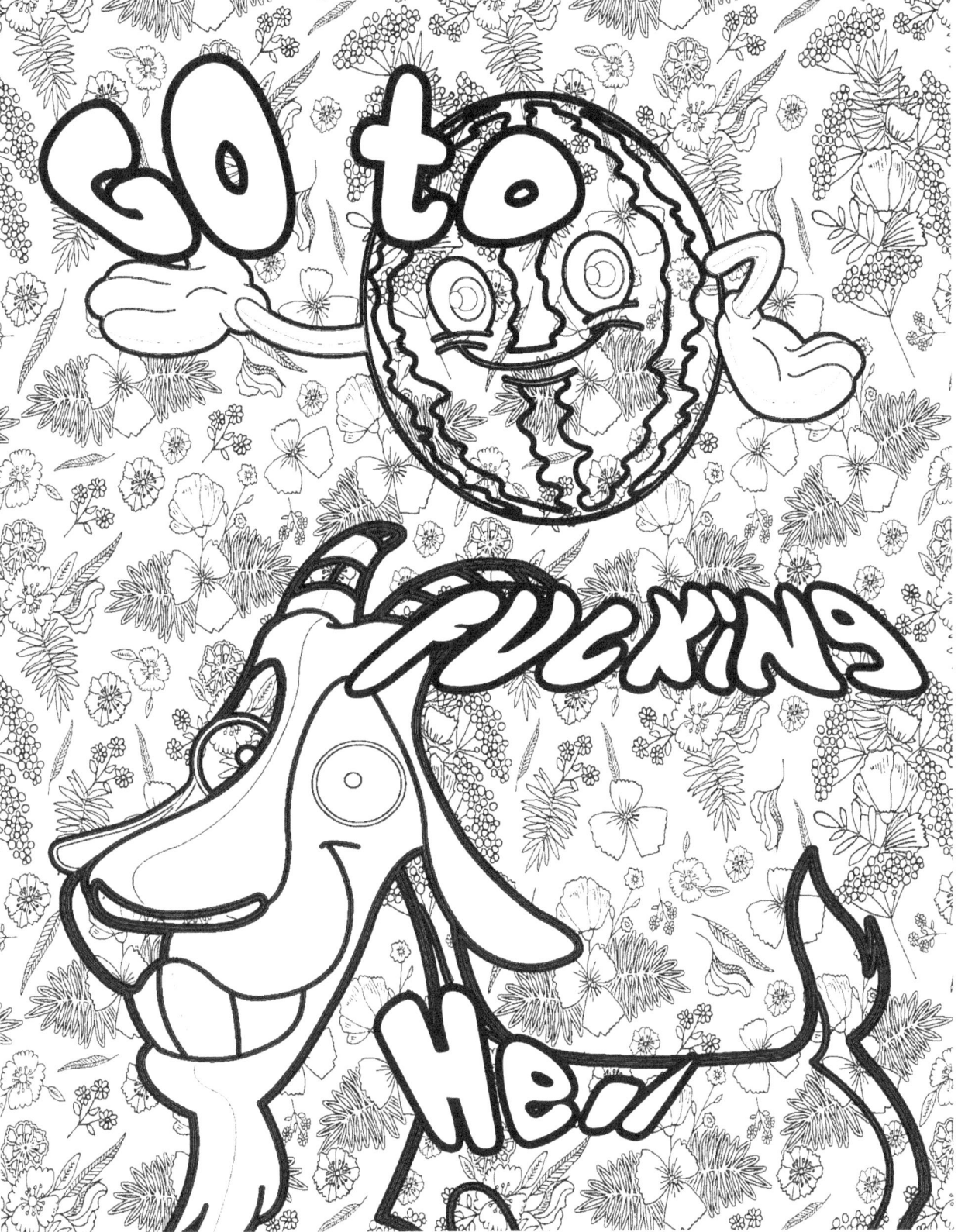

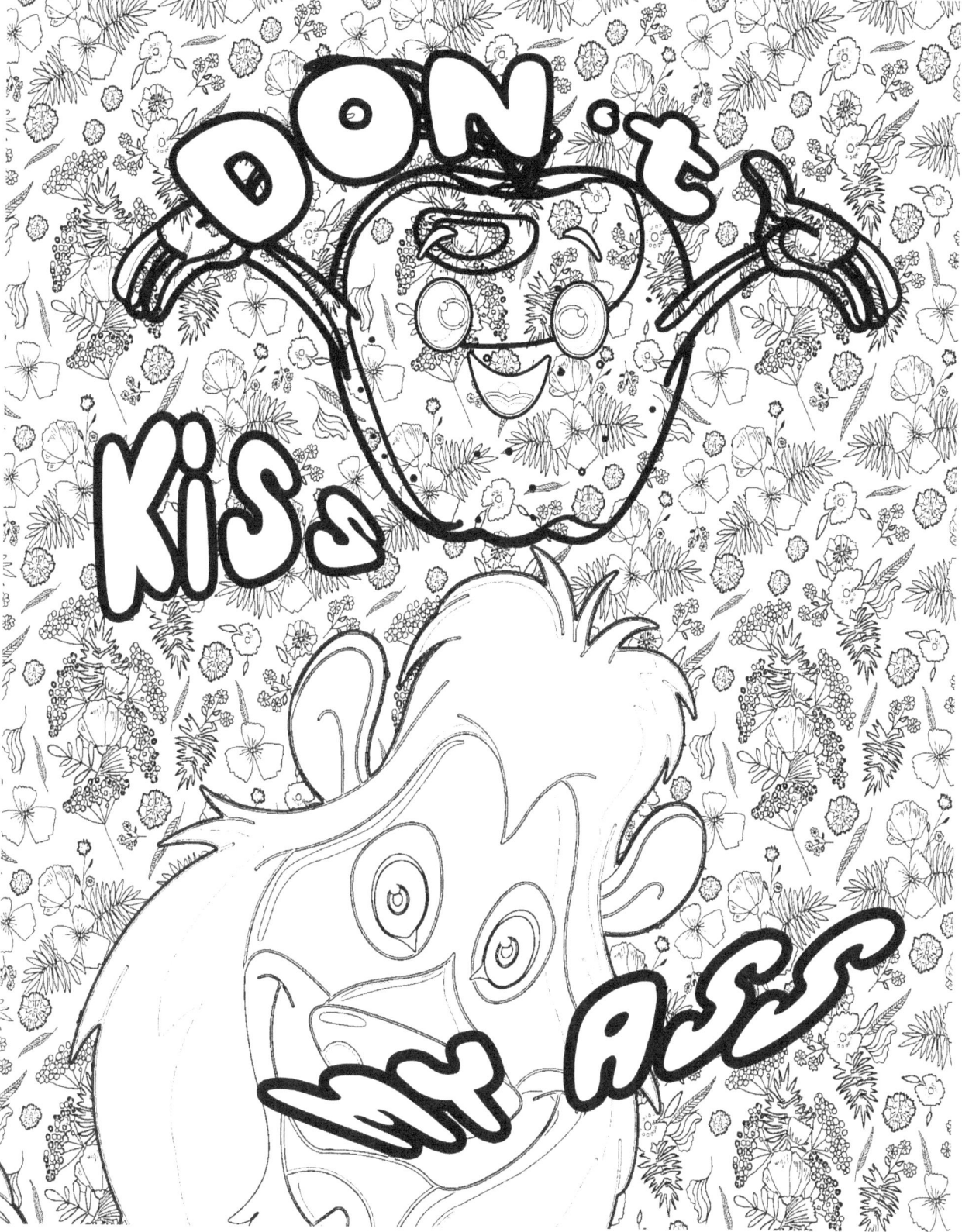

Note

www.ingramcontent.com/pod-product-compliance
Lightning Source LLC
Chambersburg PA
CBHW081122180526
45170CB00008B/2968